Wired for Hope

Wired

for

Hope

A collection of essays, poetry
&
momentary musings

Nedda Simon   Pam Horwitz

Edited by
Barbara Prendergast

Photographs by Julie Grady

Blue Horizon *Publishers*

Illinois

Published by Blue Horizon Publishers, Tiskilwa, Illinois.

Printed by CreateSpace

Design by Pamela Horwitz

Edited by Barbara Prendergast

Select Photographs by Julie Grady

Additional photographs available in the public domain or are licensed for use by Pamela Horwitz and Nedda Simon

Wired for Hope/by Nedda Simon and Pam Horwitz

ISBN 13:978-0692817605

First Edition

To our families, friends, and a community of women.

Contents

Introduction

This book is a collection of essays, poetry and momentary musings that focuses on how women respond to life crises and the events that can define them and shape their futures. However, men can certainly find tools in these pages to guide and support them -- when all seems to have come to a stop and there are no paths to follow forward. Join us as we explore the whole spectrum of life's challenges, and messages of hope. *We believe to seek recovery means to heal ourselves and to revive our spirits.* Find the strength and energy within you to make the changes that give your Self serenity, peace, and joy.

Messengers that step onto our life paths will tell us something we need to hear or know. These messages are not only valuable, but can be lifesaving. Nedda Simon and Pam Horwitz have known and shared a path of recovery and friendship for over 30 years. Our personal experiences only strengthened the belief that we are all *Wired for Hope,* -- a message we felt we needed to share with other women. We are grateful for the advice, mentoring, prayers, friendships and love offered to us through our own life journeys and during the writing of this book.

A Message from Nedda (N)

I always understood that I could reach for the stars. Growing up on a family farm taught me the value of hard work. My family relied on gratitude as their life's compass and taught me that a strong personal foundation and success was built upon faith, courage, and hope. I grew up knowing that regardless of tough times, all would be well.

My professional path as a counselor of chemically dependent women and those who had been emotionally and/or physically abused; a teacher; public speaker and life coach has taken me around the country to share the message of strength, recovery, and hope. My professional philosophy and humble belief in the power of hope, allowed me to earn the trust of my clients; to walk together with women in crises as they began and then fulfilled their own journey of recovery.

Through my work, and as I share in my essays and musings, I know first-hand the despair; fear; and sense of failure that comes from emotional, physical, psychological, and spiritual pain. I know that personal sorrow can plunge someone into their darkest of days described in *"A Look at Grief and Depression"*; and that sometimes, the choices made can be desperate and ill-measured, such as found in *"Emotional Health"* and *"Where Do We Go from Here?"*

Fully understanding the need to assist clients with life's challenges and self-discovery, I continued to learn and rely upon the wisdom of my own guides and messengers of hope – *"Spiritual Health and the Beliefs That Matter"*. Throughout the years, my own professional path included the shared insights offered by mentors, other counselors, pastors, family, and ultimately, to rely on an inner strength gained from the power of prayer and meditation.

A Message from Pam (P)

I speak and write to my experience as a woman in recovery. With family roots in the rural Midwest, I grew up believing that one must work for what one wants; believing in the fundamental idea that anything is possible; and only limited by my own expectations. I understood that someday I would likely arrive at a crossroad -- or a time and place in life when I would need to make positive changes.

For me, this meant that it was important to: leave no stone unturned; define myself in society; and to live a life with purpose. Over the years,

I shared my experience with other women in recovery, demonstrated the willingness to seek a better way of life and took personal, life-changing risks with confidence and courage.

I often reflect on the steps I took that brought me to this day: I knocked on the door and was greeted with the confident welcome, "I've been waiting for you." It was Nedda Simon: counselor, mentor, and friend, described in *"The Skeleton Key I"*. That was the first day of my own recovery. I learned I was addicted to alcohol and recovery was more than putting the cap on the bottle. I learned that treating my addiction was just the tip of the iceberg.

I soon learned how frightened and selfish I was and sadly, I did not have a clue who I was. I quickly learned there was some very hard work ahead and relieved to learn that I had a partner with whom I would travel the path of recovery. I was relieved and grateful to learn that there was hope and looked forward to the day when I knew I would be strong enough to walk the path for a while, alone.

I describe my first steps toward self-discovery in *"Soul Speak"*, and offer lonely insights on personal shame in *"…Cat's Song"*. I look deep and share the feelings of fear and my new-found, unspeakable shyness in *"Stage Fright"*. I share a piece of my story in the poem, *"Let's Go Home"*, where I explore the world around me and finally, come home, feeling whole.

You see, addiction, abuse, fear, and loss will hold you hostage if left unchecked. We invite you to explore the story of our shared journey of recovery in *Wired for Hope*. We invite you to walk the path of self-discovery with us as we share recovery insights in our essays, poems, momentary musings, and helpful tools that encapsulates the ups and the downs of every-day life. Discover the possibilities that are out there for you and learn that life can offer serenity, peace, and joy. Moreover, we believe that you will find the courage to reach deep within yourself, and know that you'll discover a future full of hope and tell a story of your own.

Cobwebs

The humidity hung in the air and created a haze over the crops in the morning cool. As she walked she saw there were thousands of little webs. Some a foot wide; all part of the same crocheted pattern.
Tiny circles knitted outward. Some were draped like jewels on a silver chain with the center swaged by the weight of the dew.

Each spider had anchored the work at the top of prairie bluegrass stems, two single strands swung over like cables for the beginning of a magnificent bridge in a harbor. Single strands holding the load of the precious artwork.

Each foot or so of bluestem held one of these doilies. So, fragile, yet strong in their world. Reminding us of our own structures of strength seemingly fragile at times—holding us in the tough times.

Nedda

Wired for Hope

Sometimes, as humans, we try to make sense of the insanity around us. We know things aren't right, or we're having a strange experience while those around us act as if everything were normal. We work hard at trying to either correct it, go along with it, or resign ourselves to the situation.

This is where human nature to feel hopeful comes in. We just know things will get better; or we question if we could be wrong about our conclusions of the world around us. Well, we have every right to question what's going on around us. When our self-esteem, confidence or spirit is challenged, stand firm.

We all know those who stood firm about what they believed and who spoke up or worked to change themselves or the situation. Changing our circumstances or ourselves is the beginning of healing from any trauma.

A person who is severely injured hopes to get out of the present situation and then works hard to get well. The injured person sees this as a terrible situation that makes no sense, but he or she begins to work toward the future immediately. The person fights to live, with small goals at first; his or her view widens as this person works on recovery and perhaps, although not completely the same as before, he or she becomes whole.

You may not be able to change the things around you, but you certainly can change yourself and your viewpoint. This is recovery. This is getting well. This is change for the better and for you as an individual.

Let's be clear about one thing. Not everyone will think your personal changes are great. Some people will feel a shift in the relationship with you that they may not like, and it will make them very uncomfortable. For example: if you lose weight, some people will try to get you to eat more, exercise less or dismiss the whole plan you've developed. Remember: this is your life and no one else's. *N*

Our struggles; our stories;
our recoveries --
all as old as man himself.

Pam

Soul Speak

It was the first draft,
an ever changing
life script. Letting
go, letting my guard down, giving in
to the desire of which was absolutely
prohibited. Odds were,
I was blindly walking
right into the red-light district of my soul.
The provocation –
all colorful characters take residence there.
According to some, according to my mother,
I was exposing the red-light story line.

What I found there:
A family circus in not just the living room,
secrets and skeletons
all dressed up in Sunday's best,
an alter ego-centric
Achilles' heel and the many shoes that fit,
a big, black light
illuminating every slinky shadow,
every sleazy stain
including all the sorry, sultry nights.
Sadly,
Mom was right.

Like a moth to the flame,
I faithfully hovered
around a new bright light, drawing on
its necessary sustenance.
I searched further for the vital heat,
and I took my soul-fight into the street.

An ugly scene for all to see.
Raw, fragile, bruised from my first go around,
it was time for a new story line, the second draft.
Moreover, a change in course; breaking free.
Fearless, I rushed in headlong
to dismantle; extinguish the old ways.
Healing, seeking, speaking.
P

It Seems to Me

When we are born, we are spiritual beings and have wisdom. Then, the world begins to train us in the ways it knows. We have a name, a given identity and soon we must learn the world's way.

We lose our mastery of Self. We have only one life or personhood. It's our own Self. Not someone else's description and it is not someone's description of our life.

We must stop seeing ourselves as a possession in the 21ˢᵗ century.

Others place an identity upon us and tell us what and who we are. We learn danger and mistrust. We lose the safety promised by the family. As we grow older, we learn how to cope. Alcohol, gambling, cheating and manipulation help us to fight our way through the world. We feel the first losses and experience painful events. Children and adults alike learn ways to weave their way through tragic and painful experiences.

Something happens that can draw us to realize we can't go down this road anymore. Destruction is near and that ancient urge to be a spiritual being again comes. We ask for help. This is the beginning of recovery and a renewal of the real self you were supposed to be.

Oh, you will be human, but better, kinder, more loving to others, less selfish and willing to learn what it takes to be whole. Your outlook will be positive, you will make plans for your future and maybe do something that you have always longed to do, but didn't know it -- because someone told you that you couldn't.

Recovery begins with surrender of all old notions, beliefs, labels, and identities that have been given to you. You throw away all you ever knew about anything and everyone to see the truth about yourself. Inherently, you are wired for hope and can now begin to build yourself, discard old habits and beliefs about how you should live. If you are quiet enough and stop listening to the world's racket, you will hear your Voice.

The universe teaches the sounds of your own Voice through the rustling of leaves, the brilliance of the sunset, the splash and feel of the water on your face. You will become alive like a newborn; but this time, you will resist the outside noise and build a new way to see and feel the world around you. *N*

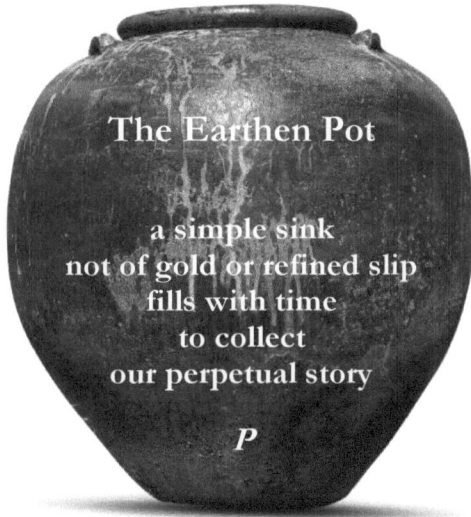

The Earthen Pot

a simple sink
not of gold or refined slip
fills with time
to collect
our perpetual story

P

When the Monkey Plays

In the monkey's hands, the wheel sings
with weird laughter.
Spinning faster, an old spun web
complicates my thoughts,
each knot drawn
tighter and tighter, the hangman's noose.

I cannot catch my breath. Black,
blue, dancing
in the hard acid rain as it pours
out of my hand, apologies
do not work in this rhythm;
time better spent when you did not know me here.

When the darkness had been the pathway, a strange geometry --
twisted and crooked,
familiar. It is true,
the devil's tongue had seared his brand.
Pan, I played his flute,
carried his tune through the fields.
A true nature: hidden, wet and slithering along,
found against the edge of the stream.

Cold to the bones, I beckoned the day
light to bring relief
as the season was waning,
long endless nights were soon, gone.
At last, a purgatory, the cliché of a stolen kiss of my own, at dawn.
Or, perhaps this time,
an eternal bye.

I do not know what I will find in this new playground.
P

Recovery

We believe to seek recovery means to heal ourselves and to revive our spirits. We needed to heal emotionally, physically, psychologically, and spiritually. We wanted to heal; we searched for relief from the painful circumstances that life had dealt us, painful experiences of our human condition. In the past, we tried to mend, mask and escape that condition by shutting ourselves down. We discovered that our failed attempts to heal led to even more painful outcomes and only offered a temporary fix; a bandage; a short-term answer to a long-term problem.

Recovery too, is part of the human condition. We're wired for hope and our god, our higher power, our universal goodness wants us to heal, to be whole; to be whole in spirit. The path of recovery offered us more than just a short-term answer. We found success in healing painful wounds; we found success in making our lives meaningful and once again, whole. *P*

Prayer

Thank you for the soaring eagle,
the prairie grass and the mountain brook racing to the sea.
Give us wisdom
to preserve all of Mother Earth's Treasures
and Father Sun's Life Force.
Let us bring peace to others and
bless all the bounty you provide.
Amen.

Nedda

God Wants Us Whole

The image of being a whole person is so comforting. Yet, we humans can be willful. This blocks our search for any kind of spiritual quest we attempt.

Being stubborn – resisting any new ideas, or deciding our way is the only way – creates obstacles and goes in opposition to our true selves when God might be trying to talk to us. Regardless of our concept of a god, we can't learn unless we become open and willing to hear. Willfulness comes out of fear. It is the idea of holding on to the rope, because we might fall if we let go.

In recovery, your first job is to let go of the rope of old beliefs. This takes some doing. Take your time and don't tell anyone since each person, bless them, will try to give you their ideas. Each of you must take this journey alone. Sometimes you see a person's attitude, his or her seemingly peaceful outlook on life. Explore what that person knows and believes and see if it fits for you.

New songs come to you from The Spirit. Sing, drum, dance, talk. Say the words you hear. Don't be afraid. New songs are there – listen. *N*

Becoming humble allows you to let go of self-importance.

New songs come to you from The Spirit. Sing, drum, dance, talk.

Nedda

Bare. Stone. Cold.

The bare stone
felt cold.
The rug pulled out
from under me.

Hard,
life. Lucky,
I did not hit my head.
Crazy enough. How do I know
-- she said,
I am rational? Weird
thing to say.

Nothing,
down to nothing, to rebuild
again. Bare stone.
Cold.
P

Surrender. Let go of old beliefs, a vacuum of new thoughts and new beliefs will rush in. Now is the time to surrender.

Life
makes us blind
to simple truths
and stops the flow of all that is creative.
Nedda

Balance in Our Lives

I hear the constant complaints about stress. "I'm stressed out; I'm unable to get anything done." "Life is confusing and complicated." "So many responsibilities, so little time. I don't have time for myself; I'm just so busy with everything."

Balance is a useful word; but how does one get it? Establishing balance in our life comes with examining four aspects that play a key role: emotional, mental, physical, and spiritual.

We can easily check out our physical health: diet, weight, exercise plan and so on. We can have someone whom we trust tell us how we're doing emotionally. Make sure our social life is contributing to our overall well-being.

Our spiritual life is an essential piece of a balanced life, and it is easily overlooked or ignored. How do we think of ourselves in relation to others, the world, and the universe? What do we believe in, who do we trust to be with us when everything seems lost?

Spirituality is a sense of oneness with the world around us – a connection with the universe. We are "the stuff of stars". Science and religion coincide to make our lives make sense. There doesn't have to be a conflict with those who have faith – in God, let's say – and in science. Science explains the processes of the universe and makes it more wonderful.

Learning more about other religions and the explorations of the universe makes each of us more understanding, open to diversity and human beliefs. There is no balance in us if we refuse to learn anything new about others or the world.

Believing in a higher power or a powerful entity will help you not to be so important all the time. Stress comes when it demands endless action, opinions, and decisions.

Believing you are everything to everybody is not only exhausting but arrogant.

Having a quiet place to go in your mind, where you can get your bearings, breathe, and feel a sense of connection with something greater than yourself, is not only smart but also can save your sanity and your life. Meditation, prayer, or just quiet time to think of a strength that sustains you can be done at your desk, at home or at play. It quiets your mind and gives you a different view of your surroundings. Someone yelling that a report is due will get you back in perspective.

A spiritual life gives you a sense of value when you are feeling inadequate. You are contributing; you are a part of the universe; you do matter; you do care about the well-being of others and the world.

You will like being around those who have spiritual lives. They are calm, centered, loving, honest, and straightforward in their relationships.

To become a spiritual being, you must recognize your inclusion in the whole – not the center of the whole – but the world and all life in it. What a glorious concept! What peace can come when everything seems out of balance. You can step back, pause, and say, "All will be well." *N*

Admit you are scared.

Shells

We walk and pick our shells. We bend and peer intently;
finding one that seems different calls for an assessment.
"Look at this, what do you think? Oh, keep it! What about this one?"

We search, find, assess, enjoy, discard and keep. This is a familiar task.
Throughout our lives this exercise has been repeated over and over.
Looking out from our marriages, our friendships, our families;
picking our way, discarding what has hurt or
keeping the broken chards in a way to heal.
Enjoying the very best of the treasure
to sit on the shelves of our days.

Nedda

Photo courtesy Julie Grady

There is a saying in Tibetan,

"Tragedy should be utilized
as a source of strength."
No matter what sort of difficulties,
how painful experience is,
if we lose our hope,
that's our real disaster.

Dalai Lama

Photo courtesy Julie Grady

Stage Fright

Not a sound, trapped
at the gate, a grim calm.
No appeals heard with a fool's painted tongue
in this clown's court. Defects
raging, amplified in the stillness.
I twist and struggle to
sip from the seep;
a spout
dribbles close to the pipe.
I am so thirsty.

I cannot pray for grace here,
in this place, found at the end
inside these narrowing walls, a locked exit.
I seek a dim light, a small crack,
a different door
that will swing the other way.
Slow closure, desperately
certain after the audience celebrates.

I do not know anyone here.
They stop to listen, then, laugh-out-loud
in muted parody at my obvious verbal-less contortions.
Cowards believe they are powerful,
they take hostages.
Weak now, I fall to my knees to repent --
my solo, without a song.
P

Hope is the only thing stronger than fear.

A Closer Look at Fear

Fear is a built-in survival tool. We hate the feeling of it and will try anything to avoid being afraid. Just think of all the things that can scare us. Any change in our routine can make us nervous. For some of us, meeting new people, moving to a new place, or changing jobs is enough to make us not even consider making a move forward. We will even put up with awful situations before changing. We can learn to adapt to frightful environments. Domestic abuse is a striking example.

We know the "fight or flight" instinct is ancient and can save our lives. Left over from prehistoric times, it tells us to act. Now, we can't pick up and throw our spear or run from our boss's office. We are left with stress. Our blood pressure goes up, we feel ill and we have no way to diffuse this natural response.

We have a way out of this modern mess. We need to stop and see what is making us so fearful. Of course, our instincts should be alert in dark parking lots, but usually we have some time to think about our fears. In normal circumstances, what scares us is not really that threatening.

A new job is a wonderful opportunity to personally grow. Changing your attitudes and beliefs is another thing altogether. "What will my friends think if I quit drinking?" "What will my parents say if I file for divorce?" or "What will my spouse do if I quit my job?" "What will happen to me if I rethink everything I ever believed about my marriage, job, friends, relation and my life!"

I will be alone in the world and no one will come to help me.

Your mind can go haywire. It is time to stop those thoughts, slow down and realize not everything has to be done at once. Sure, this will take some courage, but you can do this and you are not alone. Many others have made these moves. Seek out those people; listen and learn.
Read on, dearest friend. **N**

It's Five O'clock   Somewhere

C   directly
to the rabbit hole
there will be no looking back --
only looking in
bound for the secrets found in the base
to extract the real.
Straight down, illusions
carry me in, across
the playing field, into the clearing
where rabbits with tall hats and batons parade in the sun,
azure blue-colored butterflies float above the whirling meadow
breeze. Wandering, searching the spirit
does not call out. Secrets
elude me in this zenith.
Alice,   are you watching me?
Slipping, sliding,
falling down…there
will be no looking back.
I will not poke the snake;
lust for the toad;
taste the forbidden this time around.
Crossing the boundary, the lines of
whimsical wishes, so tempting to: descend the stairs;
scale the castle; enter the seven mansions
anticipating ecstasy;   lift the chalice.
The clear-cut, looking-glass bottom   sparkles
at the same time each day, and
when the clock runs out
it too, will shatter. Collecting my sanity.
P

Where Do We Go, from Here?

Bewildered and confused. The longer we have struggled with our personal demons or ongoing personal pain, the more we can feel lost and alone. We grasp at anything that might make our misery lessen. We have realized we are in crisis. We are confused and scared, but we also know that everything we have tried has not worked. Advice flows from all directions, and the loneliness does not go away.

Making a change is scary enough, but friends and family can get very nervous as we show signs that we are beginning to change habits and thoughts. Most of them already may have suggested we "do something"; but when we do, they become uncomfortable and we may feel more alone. Be cautious with whom we share our intention to find a different path. Now what? With no one to go to and not being able to live on our wits and luck, we try something new.

When you feel unsafe and are not finding any more tricks to pull out, looking outside yourself just might work. Seeking the aid of a higher power takes you out of the middle of decisions. Asking for help from someone stronger, wiser, and more powerful than anything else might be the answer.

Recognize the powerlessness in your life.

This decision can make you feel less alone and more a part of a new whole world. Hope and humility come to reassure you the future can be like the ancient promise from so long ago. Once you have made the decision to let go of your life to a god you can understand, you become open to listening and learning.

This news comes in small and surprising ways. People will say things to you that you have never heard before. The world will reveal new sights; even sounds may be different, your curiosity is piqued, and you will want to know more and see more. That awful heaviness begins to fade; others' words will make sense and you can apply them to your own life. Step by step, day after day, hope gets stronger. With encouragement from others, you try harder. *N*

Wired

Humanity: connected
by chronicles of sheer will; our stories
strung together by the sinew of stars;
the strength of our hope held steadfast
by the possibilities that pour from the sky, then rise
once again with the smoke of the fire.

Hope cannot be easily vanquished, instead
it becomes a gentle flowing river of reliance,
we draw continuously from this perpetual, innate vein,
this river of hope, the water, our life-blood carries us --
we're connected by living tributaries
destined and wired for hope.

Then, hope is the creator of all that we can be,
dependably placed there; reinforced
by the toughest of times,
grounded in faith for the faithful,
set in stone for the willful.
Our foothold on hope,
is our humanity, our core assurance
that we are wired.

Connected and connected and connected.

Something more can be found here,
a self: centered, safe and rock solid;
built to withstand the test of life
and time; enduring
success, then failure, and then again…
we are destined and wired for hope.
P

All that I am or ever hope to be…

*Sometimes against all odds, against all logic,
we still hope.*

Emotional Health

Emotional health is a sense of well-being. It means feeling good about ourselves in all areas; knowing who we are, feeling good about others and the relationships we have with them. We gain a sense of power and support in times of stress and emotional upheaval.

We are able to soothe ourselves and experience hope. We have a sense of control, tempered with humility. We learn to express our feelings calmly and from our hearts.

We reveal our emotional well-being by our reactions to major life events and in everyday living. We see others behaving in a calm manner during a very stressful time and we realize that this is one of the tools we can use to see just how well we are doing as we travel our life-long journeys.

How do you want to react to a stressor? How can you get a center of calm and maintain it?

You assume you are okay emotionally, but to examine your whole self, it is important to check some emotional issues you may be experiencing. You can ask these questions: am I anxious and nervous most of the time? Am I sad? Have I lost interest or energy that I used to enjoy? What makes me happy? Do little things cause me to be angry? Do family members make comments about my anger?

Do I cry more easily or more often than usual? Do I enjoy being around family and friends, or would I rather just stay home alone on the couch? These questions can help you decide if you need to seek help.

Have you been honest with yourself? Do you see some signs that you could be more at ease with your life? If so, that realization will help you get and keep a balanced emotional life as you travel on your journey of discovery. There is no stigma in taking care of yourself in all aspects of your life. It is self-discovery. *N*

Ask questions. You don't know, what you don't know.

Resentment

One of the ways to harbor anger is to hold on to resentments. Oh, those great inventions of the mind and heart! We can invent hundreds of them. As we age, resentments get longer, deeper and placed upon more people and events.

This is not funny for anybody, it's a condition that plagues us all. We have justification for a lot of our resentments. We have been hurt or cheated in some way, or we had something go badly with seemingly no way to change it. We can hold onto these thoughts and not make any progress. We also have opportunities that were overlooked, or we regret not taking a risk. We can blame ourselves or others for our failures for years. *(You can fill in your own blanks here.)*

Have any of those bad feelings changed things for you? Have the hours spent mentally fussing with them changed the past in any way? Probably not, nor will they in the future,

Think about an instance you really were spending all your energy and time, perhaps even crying, or cursing about the person who has hurt you so badly. Now, think about what he or she is doing at this moment. Is that person feeling badly; or is he or she working, playing with the kids, or eating a nice dinner? Let it go! Don't harm yourself anymore.

Clean up your thoughts and urgings and wish those folks well in their lives! Life should be full of kind thoughts and doing good things. Resentments can make you sick physically and mentally. What a waste of time and energy. Take a deep breath and exhale those resentments into the universe where they can be dispersed with no harm done. *Forgive yourself and others, it's time to celebrate living.* **N**

Forgive yourself and others.

Life is Too Precious

Life is too precious to squander on anger. Sometimes when we are angry, it's because we're afraid. Most of us don't want to admit we get scared when confronted by new situations or when we find we must change our way of doing things.

If we admit it, anger really is upsetting. If can fester and grow into a personality that no one can like. It literally can make us sick.

Take a breath.

No one suggests that we should not be angry or express anger, but it might help if we step back a moment and ask ourselves: what is scaring us? When injustice and cruelty are present, anger is appropriate and calls for action of some kind.

We can see new things as a loss, a failure to run our own lives. This, of course, is counter to having mastery of our lives. This can be very scary, but it also might be that we are scared because we don't have mastery of anything!

Rebellion rests just beneath the surface of us all, waiting for a cause or slight or something different to latch onto. You may think, "this really makes me mad and I'm not going to take this any longer." Okay, what's your hurry!? Figure out the problem and if this is what is scaring you. If it is, be very careful. You can get yourself into a lot of trouble, and sometimes irreparable harm can be done. *N*

**Don't let defeat, loss or failure run your life –
it is counter to your true Self.**

It's A New Day

Blue lies
lazily upon the horizon,
it's a new day.
I feel the fresh, warm breeze
against my face as I look out
to greet the summer morning's sun.
The garden is full of vigor, my piece of Eden -- it is
life's design.
Turns out, there are no real rules
to be imposed here, my hand
is so small here. In homage,
I am so small, am I the stuff of stars or dust?

I stroll to the edge of the nearby woods
to sit and wonder. Quiet rustling, a whispering stir,
in the otherwise still-center
of my new dewy hostel
nestled near the edge of the woods.
I catch a glimpse of a little eft as it skips
across the wet forest path beside me.
Could it be the totem calling? A familiar,
prudent voice speaks to me
while resting in this woodland refuge.
Yes, a familiar voice, in what seems a familiar and safe place.
This is the spot. I can rest, finally set my earthly bags down;
I will reside here, settle in, near the edge of the woods.

My thoughts give way to the most natural high.
They will carry me further and further,
deeper into the woods where the mysterious
business of the day is simple, complete.
Oh, at times, it is a flurry -- a scattering
of this and that, all carried out under the arboreal cloudland
canopy that protects us. Can the mystery of this, and that,
really be explored here in the woods?

Are the answers to every question, just words,
hiding needlessly beneath the woodland debris,
or camouflaged by fallen leaves? Will marked and meandering
trails, with many little moss-filled cracks, guide me on my way?
I think so. I will do my part to search
every sylvan nook to seek the Mother's secrets and
every day, I will remember
to count my many gifts, the promises made to me.
P

Photo courtesy Julie Grady

Cleaning the Closet

Emotional health begins with an inventory of ourselves. It requires vigorous scrutiny and can be a daunting undertaking if we can't think about it in simple terms. Cleaning a closet comes to mind.

We usually take everything out of a closet we are going to clean. We should think about how we will use this "closet" in the future. How do we want it to look; and what is all this stuff we have kept anyway?! Our lives, can be seen as this closet, and we can be firm about what we want to keep and what must go away.

What will stay in our lives and what must go? What fits us, and what is too old and tired? What do we love and what seems unnecessary now? Are some of our friends or family members toxic to our growth and happiness?

Are we being honest with our doctor, friends, family and at work? Are we being honest with ourselves? We can keep the "cute little dress" or the "favorite tie"; but do they fit in our circumstances now? We probably can't go back to those good old days, but we can be happy again.

37

Happiness and hope come for different reasons, but we can be sure our emotions fit our reality. As we seek feelings of safety, comfort, and hope, we throw away negative images, feelings, and regret. We forgive ourselves and throw out any damaging statements and hurt, since they keep us stuck in the past. We will keep supportive friends who are willing to accept our values and stay away from those who expect us to abuse our bodies, values, and our spirits before they will love us. It is enough to know we have begun to clean. Some things in this place will take some consideration, and certainly love and compassion, as we make changes in our "people, places and things".

Some of this will be very hard to do, but you are up to it. Don't sell yourself short. Know that you are important to many and very precious to others. *N*

Stay in reality -- live in the present, it will ground you.

Captiv-ating

The long white gloves fit perfectly
over the scars,
your slender, bruised shoulders bear
a refined ease,
sparkly nail heads are the perfect cover.
Short cropped hair does the job --
hides all
the messiness.
Your dark glasses
will not reveal the wild, painful
stare as the radio blasts the news, or
when they say, "go this way."
Your pointy-toed slides will come off your feet
if you run. Stay here,
sit quietly. We'll have a tea party.
Do you take yours with sugar?
One lump or two?
The crocheted-lace cloth covers the table,
zig zagged scratches
are cut deeply into the wood.
Madness becomes you, dear.
P

Search and find yourself. Remember, God wants us whole.

Finding Yourself

Each of you has only one life, or personhood. This is your Self, and not someone else's description of you. You may not realize this until you are in a crisis of some sort – maybe you become a victim of domestic violence; or you have begun to let go of your values and have started abusing drugs; or you are slowly becoming a gambler who loses all control; or a crisis occurs in the family.

A circumstance can interfere abruptly with the life you are living. Now you need to do something. You become more alert and aware, almost near panic. You realize you must do something differently, and soon.

For women: This is the 21ˢᵗ century, and all women need to stop seeing themselves as possessions. As women, we need to start listening to our feelings about how people address us and treat us. We need to think about where it happens, who is participating and exactly how others perceive us. Men and women both slip into cultural roles and take their places, acting as expected and not questioning what might be wrong with this picture.

This can be hard work, but you have your whole life in which to do it.

Ask yourself: "Am I always the entertainer at the family gatherings or the chairman of all the activities? Do I always say yes when I want to say no?" Stop saying yes when you mean no.

See yourself as a picture puzzle. Do you like what you see? Okay, now imagine mixing up the pieces and starting over. This time, YOU will make the picture as you like. Aren't you curious to find out how that will look? Start with this sentence: "I am." Then say who you are by using a noun. You will find as you make a list of who you are, your awareness will grow. This becomes fun, and the list grows longer and longer.

Life can make you blind to truths and can stop the flow of all that is creative. Life's pain can dull you and make you timid. *N*

Self-growth
allows you to be the messenger for others.

The Beach, A Place to Heal

*There is no match for the powers outside my window this morning. The wind sings the song of cold and blowing
sand on the beach. The water rolls to shore in white and taupe curls. The birds press in the wind to settle again, and the lone walkers on the beach believe they will stay warm if they move fast enough.*

*Lord, I love this place. It centers and humbles me.
I want to see how I can heal some and feel whole after the long recovery of surgery. I feel close to the Presence, so that can be a beginning. I feel old, yet new and scared to learn again. We are told that recovery gets easier and the path is smoother because we know the signs of no progression. I hope that is true for me. Of course, I am the worst waiter, so this is going to be interesting. I'll just start with telling the little yellow, ugly man ego to get out.*

*I'll walk on the beach and see things that are important and learn again, that
I am not very large in the scheme of things,
and my self-pride will settle down with a dose of good old humility.
Note: Find your place.*

Nedda

Hope is looking at despair from above
and knowing it is only this time, not forever.

Waiting for the Rain

Perched on the rock's edge, waiting
for the rain to hide my tears.
I watch the clouds
merge to form one
big blanket that does not give me comfort
or keep me warm.

P

43

Meditation for You: After the Rain…

You have walked for miles in the scrubby foothills of the mountains that overlook the desert floor. It is very hot and you are very thirsty, very, very thirsty. On your journey, you have fallen, cut your knees, and scraped your elbows; there is some gravel in your right hand and it stings as you walk. The hot air on your body burns. Your feet are sore and you have blisters on your toes. The bushes and brambles have grabbed at your clothes and torn them.

It is around 4 o'clock in the afternoon…you have miles to go and, you feel despair; you see the large expanse of desert floor lying before you and know that you have miles yet to go. It seems endless, remote, and full of terror. It has no end and suddenly…yet…you see in the distance – a rainstorm coming toward you; and soon, you feel the first drops of that water on your face; and then more drops. For once, you think it is a mirage and that you are so hot…and tired…and alone in this remote and terrible place, that you are imagining it and that it is a trick of your mind.

But then, you can taste it on your tongue and it tastes sweet. Almost like life must taste. Soon your body is wet, and it starts to run down your leg and down your back and down your neck and cool your hot skin. And, the pain in your palms and your elbows and your arms where the brambles have scratched you have begun to lose their sting.

You take off your shoes and begin to run in the cool rain toward the center of that remote and scary desert; and the sand is starting to cool off on the bottom of your feet; and you run faster and faster -- your arms outstretched into the cool rain and something inside of you opens and you can see a silver cup in your mind in the very center of your being.

And the water starts to fill the silver cup, you drink the cool water, you walk refreshed and know you will remember this image as long as you live, you will be able to call up this image and take your silver cup, drink from the cup and know that someday you will never, ever be alone again, or hurt again and never again be thirsty and you will drink from this cup of everlasting life forever. *N*

A New Song

New songs come from us, from it.
Sing, drum, speak.
Sing it, beat your drum, say it out-loud!
Don't be afraid.

Nedda

…Cat's Song

She sings a desolate cat's song,
a wistful, longing cry of
solitude.
Her heart still hopes her wail is caught by the squalls to hang,
purr longer within the dark, rolling
clouds that surround her.
She touches
her tattered threads,
she gently licks her wounds. Her tender, thorn-worn flesh
is on fire with pain. She bares,
a garland of dis-grace, shame placed there
in this lonely moment of final despair.

Lastly, she reaches   calls out
to the sleeping wisdom keepers, resting
deep in the well of her being, a real
thirst to know, desire to ask for
something more: a penance.
Crescendo<, the beat of her heart drum, carries her humble song
to echo across an unforgiving wasteland;
loud vibrations of heartache
rumble and roar through the storm clouds
lifting higher…,

Awakened, Wisdom answers.
The surge rises above the stormy veil to pour the healing waters upon
her fiery flesh; to cleanse, to purify her wounds --
the stigmata
and to fill her lonely heart, her silver cup,
with mercy and grace.
P

Take a breath.

What Do We Believe, About Anything?

As you can imagine, we all possess beliefs and notions about faith; what we believe about whomever; or who is the god that we know? We ask ourselves again: What I know today to be true; do these beliefs fit? Keep in mind, we have learned religious teachings, rituals and interpretations from adults, the world around us and practices we have watched others perform. Remember the beginning where we talked about being born with so many wise and ancient teachings and the world washed that wisdom away?

We need to think as adults now and feel what is right for us as well. We must assess our spiritual lives ourselves and reflect on making it a part of a balanced life. We may discover in our spiritual inventory that we have childish notions about a god. Perhaps God has been taught as a punishing or vindictive spirit who is unapproachable or downright fearful.

We can throw away beliefs that don't help us grow and develop as caring and loving human beings and, also don't match our age, experience, or education. We don't have to believe what anyone else tells us to believe anymore!

You don't have to always have an answer.

You have the freedom to rise above the craziness around you and think more spiritually and act in a more spiritual way. You can study these concepts and they will become automatic and will give you direction in a better way.

You will keep the beautiful beliefs that inspire you to explore more about a higher power, learning how to meditate or be more creative in your prayer life. Your quest can be joyful and the most fulfilling task you will attempt. You know that your quest is carefully and lovingly watched by a Power that created the universe. A reminder that you are the "stuff of stars", making the connection again.

Working on a spiritual life will bring harmony to the other aspects of your life. You can be lean bodied and a somewhat emotionally healthy person and still feel hollow and soul-empty without a spiritual life. *This is a lifelong process.* **N**

Learn how others live spiritually. Ask what is their philosophy of life? Seek a spiritual life.

We Are Constantly in a State of Recovery

We constantly must begin again, heal again, fall or stumble again, or hope again, regain our footing or equilibrium again. The lessons in life seem to come in hardship or mistakes. That is all right. We gain something from hardship and loss. We can pass on the lessons to others to use. When we come over into the light of joy again, it is sweeter still. recovery is good, and we should not shy away from finding better ways to live.

After a crisis, we feel drained and lost. We need something constant to rely upon; a compass to help us toward the light. It won't have to be straight and narrow, or in a certain time, but a path of encouragement and hope. Living an honest and spiritual life can rid us of emptiness and loneliness.

We know how reliable the phases of the moon, the tides and the seasons are in our world. We can use those as assurances that this awfulness will not remain. We can nudge it along with a firm foundation of believing in something or someone larger than ourselves. *N*

Throw away negative images, thoughts, rules, and rituals.

You are full of unshaped dreams...
You are laden with beginnings...
There is hope in you...

Lola Ridge

Going It Alone

We read about people going into an isolated place to find themselves, to discover more about the world they live in, and perhaps to find a better explanation of life. To some of us, this sounds mildly strange to downright crazy. Then of course, there is Thoreau and his experiences at Walden Pond. I refer to that book when I feel the world is closing in and I need a refresher course in what is important and how to get back to it.

What are these people seeking? What is it that drives us to such extreme lengths to get a grip on what is important? These journeys of growing, personal development and self-crisis intervention are lonely – very lonely.

Whether we stay in our house and begin to do tough personal inventories of ourselves, our lifestyle, and all the other facets of our life and have the aid of an objective mentor or counselor, or go off to an island, we will do it alone.

Time after time, people will say, "this work is so hard and no one can do it for me or even help me." I try to assure them, but they are right of course.

Any decision, any risk, any exploration, may be suggested by someone else, but you alone take the step and alone take the consequences of the step.

This personal and solitary effort is exhilarating! By doing it, you will gain unimaginable inner strength and confidence even when you fail. You have charted a new territory, and perhaps that is what these adventurers into solitude help you to understand. When you talk about personal growth, you are going on a very solitary journey. Think about it – no one can do a personal inventory of you accurately, no one can choose to correct lifestyle habits, go on a diet, explore your God's purpose for you or decide to quit a job except you. It's understandable if you ignore the challenge or put if off. *N*

When you don't know what to do,
don't do anything.

Nedda

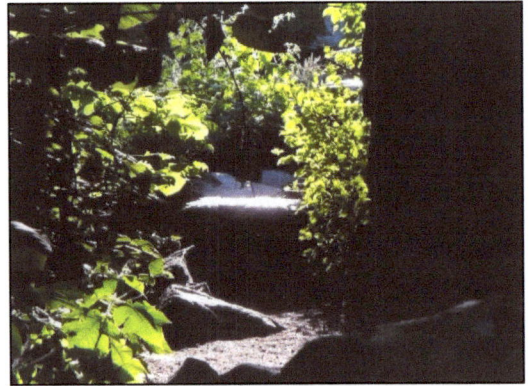

 Focus on your work, go inward to explore the real you, your needs, and desires.

The Skeleton Key I

She handed me the key,
the skeleton key.
All polished and shiny gold; only the best
attached
to the tail of her beautiful white kite.
How did she know
it would fill me with hope?
How did she know I wanted to soar;
fly away free at the end of a kite?
Fully alive. Magically
leave the world behind; to live my spirited fantasy.
New-found, vital power --
this shiny, golden skeleton key.
It fits every door. I will open them all,
like last night's glorious gross of "the Devil's Wine",
consume every, last tiny effervesce.
Boldly venture an intoxicated peek
through the keyholes,
lucky me. I catch a glimpse of what waits
on the other side;
my new-found life
in the clouds. At last,
I open a door;
I lose my grip; I miss my step.
I fall fast into a mad, mad real-life world.
My morning, noon, and night after -- full of remorse,
low with self-loathing.
She did not warn me that I could lose my grip.
She did not tell me that I would fall.
Just as quickly as I let myself go, just as quickly
I tried to hold tight
to the tail of the kite. *P*

Ask, and it will be given to you;
seek, and you will find;
knock, and the door will be opened to you.

Matthew 7:7

The Transition into Spiritual Health

How do we get to spiritual health? There is nothing more devastating for a human than when they realize there are no other solutions to the problems overwhelming them. Panic, fear, hopelessness and giving up seems the last thing to do.

Mysteriously that is the answer.

If there is no other trick to play to make us feel better, or make things work the way we want, we give up. In fact, that is good. Just give up and wait. Look around and see that the world has not ended and that things still work for others.

It must just be in *our* world. Well, what do those people do? They possibly believe in something bigger, smarter, kinder, more loving, and certainly more powerful than they are. They believe they don't have all the answers; they ask for help. They study and study, then conclude, that there is a power greater than they are and all they need to do is look and ask.

It doesn't matter what IT is called, but for this purpose, use your higher power. It can be nature, groups of people willing to help us, or a sacred place. Begin to trust this higher power: talk; share the fear and pain you feel.

Listen, the answers and thoughts will come; the right people will speak and you will get a hint of what a glorious life is out there! **N**

Let's Go Home

I was feeling confident in my choice
to move to the city, as I stood in my office
on the 6th floor of the downtown high rise. Work.
The night drew on, the backcloth,
a brightly lit cityscape.
Citified.
My thoughts, interrupted by the sound
of the Velcro that secured my bag,
separated, with one quick pull –
I swore, chased the man
to the down elevator. 911.
I went home, drove around the block,
around the block. The man stepped
into the dark crosswalk,
flash. "Zip it up!"
Around the block, around the block. I parked.
Pervert.

The short, fat gypsy woman pulled open the
purple-beaded curtain to invite me in.
She could see into her magical, crystal ball,
the wall I had just passed under
the train stop.
There was graffiti scribbled there for me
to read.
Ne portez pas de cuir et de peuplement à l'feu stop!
Don't wear leather and stand at the stop light!
I loved her
colorful turban.

I wandered over to the hippie café,
sat down to read

the leftist propaganda,
drink the free trade coffee, alone.
They were playing Go in the dark cafe
around the corner. I don't play Go.
The young server, dressed in black, nose pierced.
Jeal-ous.
I had mine done at the nearest, cleanest tattoo
parlor, next to the store that sold fun sex toys.
I think I'll write poetry, garden
the rest of my life. Maybe cook exotic foods,
when I have more time. L'ennui.

I took my new-found-self to heart, then
traveled on my way.
Not by train, as I prefer to drive. The next stop
on my journey uptown, was a visit
to the little shop that belonged to Dr. Woo.
Wowed
by the apothecary jars
lining the walls from floor to ceiling.
The clear glass jars
held all the secrets to a good long life.
Woo had just finished teaching a class
in swords. "No acupuncture today.
In the brown paper bag, try a mix of this,
and that. Make tea.
Good day."

She was walking
down the street on the sidewalk
from the apartment
where Mandino says, "God lives."
Watching her,
she could not step on the cracks

or it would break her mother's back.
Her long, scraggly hair looked as wild as she,
her lonely conversation heard
throughout my neighborhood.
I anxiously asked if she needed help…
"Mind your own business, bitch!"
I was warned; do not walk one block west.
If you walk west, you learn to panhandle,
smoke cigarettes
for free.

Up the stairs, down the long hall;
my neighbor fed expensive food to her cats.
Everything I possessed was stuffed
into my studio –
I could have filled a house.
The walls, thin. Dirty. They could all hear me cry,
the roaches.
Ran errands. While I was out there was a break-in.
$400.
I could not pay the rent;
ran out of gas.
Pawned the
mabe pearls.

Broadways, urban high rises
and bungalows.
Tick. Tock. Where does time go
when you spend it
at the beach or getting a farmer's tan?
Breakfast on the porch; freshly ground,
brewed black coffee; the smell of the
newly worked soils of the garden.
Passing my days

in the moment -- I am not patient.
The workmen arrived; hurried
to repair the roof, sand the floors,
paint the walls. I took the pets to the vet.
Black berets, red lipstick, the cigarettes are free;
Saturday night
at an off-street bookstore -- eye candy for dinner;
better yet,
an ice cream social in the park.

It is late in the day.
I bought new pearls.
Looking in the store front windows,
strung along the busy, crowded street
in the city; I dreamt of far-away places.
Silken saris, curious masalas,
dewy drops of rose water,
beautiful bare feet adorned with shiny, golden jewelry.
With my shopping bag now full,
I headed home. It had been a long walk,
however, not too late in the day.
I hung the sweet silk in my windows;
I tasted the sweet and savory masalas;
made an Amish apple pie
with a few, precious drops of delicate rose water.
I treasure my tough-skinned bare feet –
they walked me home.
P

A Bird Brain

We had a storm, and I was picking up sticks in the yard,

and I found a robin's nest that had fallen out of a maple tree nearby.

It was perfectly formed. A mud bowl,

intertwined with bits of string, grass, and twigs all woven in

a perfect dimension for her eggs. A piece of pottery made with great care and skill,

just the right shape for her and her husband to nestle their brood.

Nedda

A Place of Grace

There are those who bring beauty and more.

Our home should be our shelter and our refuge. Some of us need someone to help us

bring order to our plans. After all, we need our own space to call our own.

Simple or grand, this is where those, like Connie, come to help us.

A few swatches of fabric, some drawings, and colors to consider,

she designs a place of safety, calming conversation, and quiet.

Harmony in a chaotic world outside.

A place of grace.

Nedda

I Like Love

I like love. Scientists have established that as humans we need to be loved and to love. This makes sense. We thrive when we are around people who love us, and we get a lift when we love someone or do something with love for others.

We can read the descriptions of love in every culture's literature and art. It is in some ways the impetus for all human behavior. No wonder we mess it up so many times. We have done awful things in the name of love. We have done great things in the name of love. In endless ways, humans have used it as an excuse for just about everything. Self-worth can get caught up in this as well. We see this in abuse cases, where the victim translates the periods between the episodes of abuse with true love. "Well, he tells me he loves me."

Ask yourself: Is this relationship only habit? Does it help me continue to grow? Should I marry or just date? Should I move in with my family or will I strain the precious love between us? How much do I love doing this? Can I give it up without much pain…?

Love is tricky, huh?! We are human and need love. Recovery allows us to sort it out and then enjoy life. After all, most of us have seen all shapes and sizes of it and we know love is just to be enjoyed. *So, as it has been said in ancient verse, love is kind; so, offer love.* **N**

A Fine Example

We have all met or know someone who has a special calm about him or her. If we spend some time around people like this, we begin to realize that it is more than a calmness. It is deeper and more lasting. Each time we are with them, we feel better afterwards; or, if we only see them once, we come away wishing we had spent more time with them.

What is it about these encounters that we always remember and want to repeat?

There are religious folks, but this is different. I choose to call these folks spiritual or having spirituality. I have made a list of some characteristics these folks always display.

They have good manners, empathy, attentiveness to others, and are good listeners. They don't seem to ever be in a hurry, so they seem calm and don't show stress or worry. They are kind, genuine, have a great sense of humor, and are the first to make fun of themselves. They don't gossip or have harsh remarks about others. Good news about others pleases them and they celebrate others' success. They also help others succeed and thrive.

How do we become more like these people without imitating them?

I don't believe in turning ourselves into a duplication of these people. I am suggesting if we admire these qualities, we all can develop these in ourselves. What a benefit to our families, friends, and the world if we could cause an epidemic of spirituality. *N*

A Tiny World View

*From the couch in the living room, I could see a square of window
on the stair landing. The clouds drifted by and the blue background
made them whiter still. I was trying to heal from my third hip replacement
on the same hip and I had this little window of wonder. It reminded me of
life's movement and the grace that comes with a larger view of
God's love and helped me to be patient.*

Nedda

> *I find hope*
> *in the darkest of days,*
> *and focus in the*
> *brightest.*
> *I do not*
> *judge the universe.*
>
> *Dalai Lama*

A Look at Grief and Depression

Be sure not to confuse sadness with depression, in loved ones or in ourselves. It's normal to feel sadness sometimes. Sadness can last for a few days before the afflicted person starts to feel "normal" again. In our experience, sadness over a loss or event seems to come and go – like the tide, as someone once suggested. *(I do not address the feelings upon the loss of a child. I have not had that awful experience.)*

Memories flood in, and the sadness swells and stays. After a time, a tide of sweet reprieve slowly comes and the sadness flows away. Yes, the sadness will return again and again; but as months and years go by, the force of the tide that almost knocked you down with terrible force will start to get easier to resist. It's as if we stand up better and longer to each new surge. Eventually, sweet memories and even laughter can replace the crushing pain. Depression is different. It feels heavy and relentless, not allowing interest in

67

anything or anybody. Food doesn't taste good; normal chores are hard to think about; procrastination and sleep feel good. Life has no bright spots, and sleep is full of anxiety and worry. Sensitivity and irritability come easily; the tears are always close by. It's a miserable experience.

Grief has a remembrance that every human understands. On 9/11, our nation shared a universal shock and grief; but as a nation we also are recovering and moving forward. It took a long time for life to feel safe or normal again.

Anyone can slide into depression after a grievous event. This is when others can, and should, suggest outside help. If you experience depression, you can get an assessment from your doctor. However, sometimes depression can cause its sufferers to become stubborn and resist treatment. The fear of drug addiction is an excuse; antidepressants are safe and effective. Again, talk to your doctor. Take someone with you who can help explain what he or she is observing as well. Do not listen to gossip or coffee-time talk.

Support is readily available when you are grieving, but depression can be a very lonely road. Seek help. Get good advice and follow it. *We are with you all the way.* **N**

Spiritual Health and the Beliefs That Matter

These are reflections when my spiritual health needs fine tuning. I simply try to inventory what is going on, and the following is one of those times.

Taking walks on the beach seems to ground me. I know The Spirit is with me.

I must not be glib. I must be attentive to this low ebb in the tide. I need to look out and see if I have overlooked something on the beach that I must study. Sometimes, I feel confident that I know enough about my spiritual life. Still, what makes me yearn for more? I want to know more, yet I don't study.

What is to study? What do I need to study? Where has that feeling gone; or is this like a good marriage, settled down after the heat to a comfortable, safe, stable knowing that allows life to happen with the foundation here to support it?

What do I do now? I stop and wait. Get the "I" out of sentences and see the color of that little mean man again. He sits in my middle like a bloated and gloating blob, laughing at my foolishness and knowing full well how powerful he is. It is all right. I have the warrior King who can fight anyone who threatens me. I just must put down the mask of ego and wait for instructions. What a great gift to be here on the sea and receive my instructions and ease away from such a powerful force.

If I am still, the lessons will come and all will be well.

So simple, but as humans we try to make it hard. Let the outgoing tide take away the harshness you have placed on yourself. Let the new wave bring fresh new energy and calm to you. **N**

Listen – great teachers are everywhere.
Find your higher power.
Ask for help and let the spirit come in.

69

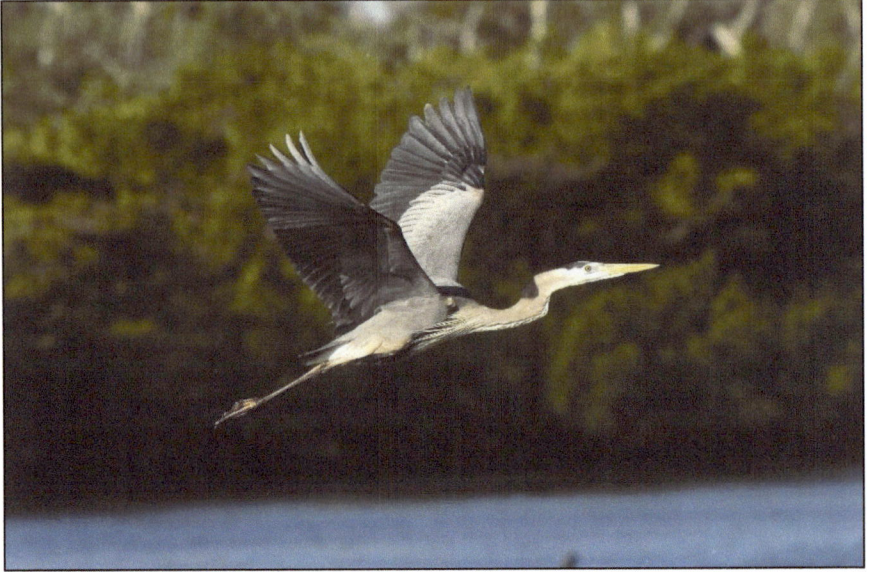

Heron Medicine

She flew
low against the headwind.
Slow, easy, purposeful.
Long enough for dialogue.

P

Don't Sing, Lori!

We say, "don't sing, Lori." The joke is on us.
The tune might not be just so,
but the lyrics come from her light within.
They tell of strength, give encouragement and hope.
Counsel we can use in our journey of crisis and triumphs.
She is always willing to share her extraordinary memory
and reminds us to laugh.

Nedda

Hope is the thing with feathers
That perches in the soul.
And sings the tune
Without the words,
And never stops at all.

Emily Dickinson

Photo courtesy Julie Grady

Hope held steadfast
by the possibilities that pour from the sky,
then rise once again
with the smoke of the fire.

P

73

Russian River

Many of us have memories of places that have stayed with us.
One of mine is a trip we took to California. Someone suggested we drive to the coast
to a small restaurant overlooking the Pacific Ocean for dinner.
The windows overlooked the entire beach
and the Russian River that ran down to meet the ocean.

The road there is winding through low coastal mountains.
The old timber bordered the road and it took a while from Santa Rosa,
where we were staying. It was sunset, and people were gathering to watch,
but they were far enough we could not know
they were building fires on the dunes
that held enough drift to block the wind and warm them.
High dunes protected the beach itself and the
fires were built on those ridges. The people looked so small and unimportant.

The red-orange circle seemed to move faster now; the sky turned to pink, purple-blue,
and as it darkened, the ocean became a slate table,
waiting for the sun to come to it in its final sigh of the day.
Now the fires began to spark and flame in the air

74

and there was the ocean, the purple river giving into it, the stretch of the dunes

framing a picture that only a Master painter could imagine.

We stood quietly.

There was nothing to say; we were subdued, by the sight.

Hold on to your memories.

They can lift you when things get tough and there seems no way out.

Bring them up and give in to a softer time and place for a while. Then, move on.

Nedda

The Imperfect Ones

Walking down to the Gulf shore was the first thing I did in the morning. I spent as much time as I could on the beach, and watching others enjoy the sea also was part of the fun. We would all stroll along. Some of us were nonchalant about our search for shells, driftwood, and other treasures. Others would take a few steps, bend over, look closely and pick, choose, sort through and toss aside those that were not just right.

Gathering our prizes was an art, we believed, and each of us had a different technique. Some of us were very discriminating. I also looked for the little shells – perhaps because I am very short, and the little ones seemed to be overlooked, and many times they were the most perfect.

Now that I think further, it makes sense that when we find a perfect specimen of anything, we exclaim, "Oh, look at this one!" We do this with people. We put them on platforms and pedestals for all to see and marvel at their perfect faces, bodies and feats of strength and athletic ability –– until they do something that disappoints us. Then they are tossed aside like the damaged shells we sort through at the beach.

How discriminating we are in evaluating shells as well as people. We have no use for the broken ones in a culture that prizes perfection. Our bodies must be slim and molded to a certain standard. We spend billions of dollars on cosmetics and clothes to bring ourselves to the mythical standard we know is valued.

To succeed – to make a mark – to be somebody – to win a trophy is part of the perfection image as well. We value the extraordinary effort. We want people to portray a life that is balanced, with no problems. We overlook the average. Average seems ordinary and downright boring.

The men or women going to a job, raising a family, paying their taxes, and attending a house of worship are not worthy of attention or scrutiny. Like a worn or less than perfect shell, they don't draw attention. They will be the "filler" in our display jar. Yet these shells and average people are who we are.

What we try to ignore or pretend we don't see is that we're all damaged, broken gifts from the sea. We need to see ourselves as part of the community of the "less than perfect". What about the imperfect ones of us, the flawed ones? We are uncomfortable and, like our own deaths, we try to ignore or pretend or don't see them or toss them aside. We must understand that to accept being less than perfect is the only way to have peace. If we cannot see the value in the broken shell, the beauty beyond the damage and scars, then we cannot truly see ourselves, nor value ourselves or others.

A broken shell has great value. It tells the story of its completeness before it ran into rough seas and rolled and scraped its way to the shore. It ran into life and suffered pain. It is no less imperfect than we are. We may be injured and perhaps broken to such an extent that we will never be the same; but we have the same value as before.

There is much relief in knowing we are not perfect and never will be! We feel a calm descend. Our life truly begins when we can forgive ourselves for not meeting the same cultural standards set by others. We can say, "This is who I am" and start to enjoy life. We can gain compassion and understanding for others, we see them with flaws and see nothing but valuable and beautiful beings. Let us see the whole little shell and value the wholeness of it all. *N*

Love Your Neighbor

A little boy sees another child sitting alone in the lunch room and moves to keep him company. A friend just gives a hug to a sad companion after hearing bad news. This is compassion.

When a friend loses a member of their family, a job, or another kind of loss comes their way, we feel sad and it is painful for us to think about their suffering. This is compassion.

We act on those feelings very often throughout our lives and little children seem to do it automatically. It sends a message of hope.

We don't have to analyze or sort out this generosity of spirit. Humans have it there on reserve. Applaud those who are generous in spirit and feel sorrow for those who can't find it in themselves. It makes our lives richer. Most are modest and don't think that their kindness and good matters, but those who receive compassion never forget it. It spreads across a community and everybody gets a boost and optimism stays a long while.

Loving your neighbor seems to work for everybody. *N*

Compassion:
the result of learning how to care for ourselves.

Pam

Within My View

Worn, chiseled, and unpolished park sculptures
not good enough to be bronze,

        cast aside

by both pigeons and passersby, but the possibilities
remain, a morsel for the empty can – cold

        stiff fingers

obediently grip yesterday's lunch,
kept warm in neighborhoods far from home.

        A stone passage

depicting a sacred ritual passed down by ancestors
each day seeking the claim of a new bench rite, the rite

        of those indigenous to insanity.

Intently, the local humanity watches the pigeons
at a food orgy, careless, the birds will leave

        today's stake within reach.

Humility no longer a virtue for those with feet
calloused by following the carved-out trails

        to now familiar sites

the sites of rambling schizophrenic speeches, made from
a stair-step stage intended for a midsummer night's dream

        in front of concrete cityscapes

that deliver ladies and gentlemen in tall office buildings,
with audiences of window washers carrying buckets

        of squeaky-clean formulas

for washing windows like camera lenses
to take still frame shots with colored film

        ignoring black and white

images that reveal stark truths.
P

Photo courtesy Julie Grady

Transitions and Phases of the Moon

Transitions in life are like phases of the moon. Here in the Midwest, one of the most beautiful times of the year is bean harvest. Just as the men are combining the fields, the harvest moon is the most stunning.

I was sitting on the porch one warm, balmy evening and the sun had just set as the huge orange moon slipped up on the eastern rim of our fields. At first it startled me. The beauty and mystery, and the uncontrollable way it takes command of the sky. Soon it was brilliant white and caused shadows on the stubble of the field. I realized that sometimes, life brings us events that I can't see coming or stop. I am in-the-midst of change. At first it doesn't seem too dramatic and it feels manageable, but I soon realize at least some part of my life will never be the same.

I can never capture that magic on the eastern porch just like that again, but it helped me see transitions in a different way. It reminded me that I was connected to nature and the rhythms of life. How precious that knowledge is. I realized although the moon was in its beautiful stage it also would go into the next phase of fading into darkness. Transitions will change me in the same way. In the darkest phases, I am forced to make tough decisions, redirect my life, say goodbye to loved ones and beloved places. Yet, there is a reassurance that I must never overlook. I will see the brightness again, directing my way, even in the dark.

I know the darkness will come. The beauty of the harvest moon is fleeting, yet all is well. The moon's cycles are a constant reminder for me. I can rely on the very rhythm of the phases. The transitions are not as daunting if I can remember that all of life is change. Nature reminds me that some things never change in the changing. I am reassured and comforted. The moon, the sun, the stars, love, bravery, loyalty, and God are all examples of permanence. Despite the phases or transitions, despite the chaos I feel as life swirls around me, making me feel lost and out of control, I can be reassured that some things are always true. The harvest moon will dazzle me again and give me beauty and rest that all surely deserve. *N*

A Robin's Nest

*This is all she needs for her brood. She can teach us
that possessions are not as important as we might think.
A few twigs; some mud is plenty for her.
We can accept what we have with contentment and gratitude.*

Nedda

The Sea and Its Lessons

I had gone out early to shell, hoping I could find the big one, the shell-find of the season, brought in the night as a specific gift for me.

There were always shells to gather, the usual mix of various shapes and sizes. I was just so sure this was the morning. After all, I was earlier than the other gatherers and I had the beach to myself.

But in the night, the tide had done different work. The ocean had carved huge dunes, large mounds with deep gullies dividing them. Remnants of the higher tide were running in troughs back to join the calmer surge. Barely a small shell showed through. The scouring had been thorough. Neither the gulls nor pipers were interested in checking for a morsel and had gathered somewhere else for their morning meals. There was nothing but smooth sand, the wind and the sun showing in the east.

No great find this morning. No showing off the sea gift to my family. I can have high expectations of how things will go and even make elaborate plans around the results. But the ancient Sanskrit says, "Plan, but not the results." Perhaps I should reframe my thinking and not get so carried away with planning ahead. If I plan into the future, I not only lose today, but the surprise of great gifts inherent in the day as well.

When I planned to find the shell, I limited the fun of hunting, the great morning air on the beach, the sight and sound of the eternal rhythms of the surf, the people strolling and the gifts the sea did offer me to keep.

We are taught early in our culture to expect a reward for even small efforts.

Better that I expect less and be open to what life offers me and relish it. The sea gave me so much that morning. First, I had never seen carved dunes before and it was so easy to walk in the hard surface that I glided along. Most importantly, it taught me the shell of the season was waiting, perhaps for me on another day; or perhaps it belonged to someone else who needed it more. *My life was full that day.* **N**

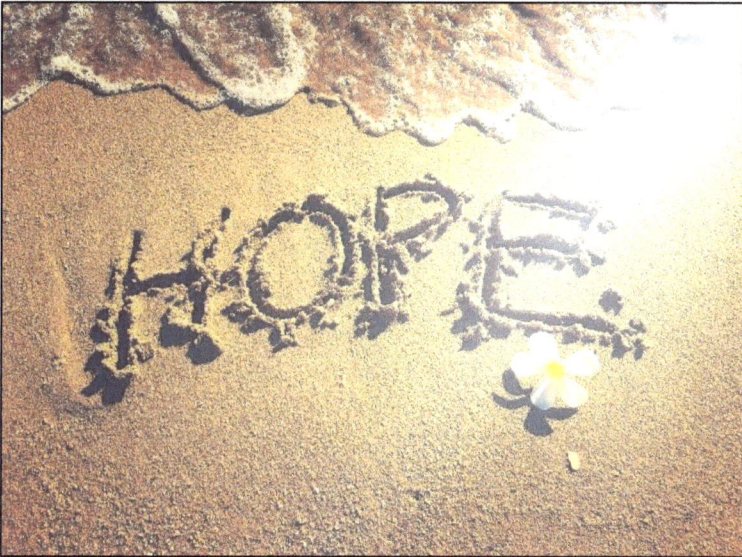

Index

Photo Credits*

Julie Grady: Photographer

Wired for Hope Cover	*Abstract Floral*	
Back Cover	*Sunset*	
	Shells	pg. *21*
	Tibetan Bell	pg. *22*
	Woodland Path	pg. *36*
	Storm Clouds	pg. *43*
	Garden Entrance	pg. *54*
	After the Rain	pg. *67*
	Fire	pg. *73*
	Harvest Moon	pg. *81*
Tool Icon	*Abstract Floral*	pp. *15,*
	17, 20, 28, 32-34, 38-39, 50-51, 54,	
	69	

* *All other photos are available in the public domain or meet the copyright and licensing requirements of third party agreements.*

Questions or comments? Contact the authors:

Nedda Simon email – neddasimon@ymail.com

Pam Horwitz email – phorwitz@yahoo.com

Blue Horizon *Publishers*

Illinois

www.ingramcontent.com/pod-product-compliance
Lightning Source LLC
Chambersburg PA
CBHW051233090426
42740CB00001B/10